Original title:
The Rhythm of One Heart

Copyright © 2025 Creative Arts Management OÜ
All rights reserved.

Author: Julian Prescott
ISBN HARDBACK: 978-3-69081-023-4
ISBN PAPERBACK: 978-3-69081-519-2

Music of Togetherness in Silence

In a room full of chatter, we silently dance,
A wiggle, a giggle, an awkward glance.
Our footsteps in sync, without missing a beat,
We laugh at our shadows, can't help but feel sweet.

With stifled burps echoing through the air,
We nod in agreement, no need to declare.
The clock ticks in rhythm, a comical show,
As we fumble and trip, putting on a grand show.

Invisible trumpets announce our parade,
Each snicker and snort in harmony made.
A duet of chuckles that never grows old,
Our silent confessions, the best tales retold.

So here's to the silence, our favorite song,
With giggles and wiggles, we joyously throng.
In the music of stillness, we find a bright start,
A symphony shared, by the beat of one heart.

Heartstrings Entwined

We danced like socks on a sunny floor,
Our laughter echoed, a heart's uproar.
You twirled, I tripped, we fell like leaves,
In this crazy rhythm, the mind deceives.

Cupcakes flew at the birthday bash,
I dodged one, but oh, what a splash!
With frosting on my nose, I grinned too wide,
This silly joy, we cannot divide.

Melodies of a Singular Spirit

We hummed our tunes on a silent street,
A cat joined in with a catchy beat.
Its meow turned into a jazzy riff,
Our hearts linked tight, in every skiff.

With kazoo in hand, we marched like fools,
Creating chaos, yes, we made the rules.
The neighbors frowned, but we didn't care,
In our melody, there's humor to share!

Pulse of an Awakening

Waking up to a snore-filled morn,
I asked my pillow: is this a thorn?
Your yawns sparked giggles, all over the bed,
What fun in this life, with dreams in our head.

Coffee spilled like a fountain of cheer,
Each sip a dance, oh dear! Oh dear!
We laughed at our clumsiness, it filled the room,
As hearts woke up to banish the gloom.

Verses of Solitary Joy

In solitude, I found my groove,
Dancing alone, my feet tried to move.
But tripped on a shoe, oh what a sight,
My solo show turned into a slight fright.

I wrote a poem with lines absurd,
Each word a giggle, not a single bird.
And in my mind, my heart gave a cheer,
For even alone, joy whispers near.

One Beat, Infinite Echoes

In a tiny town where hearts collide,
A beatbox dancer, full of pride.
He twirled and spun, quite the sight,
His pants fell down, oh what a fright!

The crowd just laughed, could hardly breathe,
As he picked them up, and did not leave.
With every thump, he shook the ground,
A symphony of giggles all around.

Harmonized Breath of Two Lives

Two friends decided on a jog,
They ran so fast, like a buzzing frog.
But half a mile, one needed a break,
Stopped for snacks and a chocolate cake.

A harmonized burp sent birds away,
As they chuckled, what a silly display.
Together they laughed, sharing the treats,
And forgot that running was meant to be sweet.

Interlaced Rhythms of Existence

Life's a dance, a wobbly tune,
With two left feet, I'll glide by noon.
Tripped over shoes and fell in style,
Got up and laughed, oh, what a while!

My partner slipped on a banana peel,
Together we tumbled, what a big deal!
We rose like stars with an awkward grace,
Dancing together, making a scene in this place.

Tidal Waves of Affection

A tidal wave of love did crash,
As jellybeans flew with a see-through splash.
We cuddled tight with marshmallow hugs,
Then bounced away on big fat bugs.

Friendship's spark igniting the air,
A tickle-fight turned into a scare.
With laughter echoing loud and clear,
We paddled on joy without any fear.

When Hearts Speak in Unison.

Two hearts in a dance, oh what a sight,
They trip on each other, then take flight.
A beat out of sync, but who really cares?
They laugh through the stumbles, swap silly glares.

Dancing with socks, left and then right,
Twisting and turning, it's pure delight.
They pant from the laughter, drop like a leaf,
In the end, they're partners in comic relief.

Pulse of a Singular Beat

With a wiggle and jiggle, they stroll down the street,
Kicking up laughter with each happy beat.
A pogo stick heart, bound for a bounce,
Their joy explodes, not one soul can pronounce.

They wear their hearts on oversized sleeves,
With playful antics, like cheeky thieves.
A chorus of chuckles fills up the air,
As they skip through the puddles, without a care.

Symphony of Solitude

A solo act turns into quite the show,
With a wink and a nudge, it's a wild glow.
One heart humming tunes, upbeat and spry,
Out pops a disco ball, oh my, oh my!

Dancing like nobody's watching at all,
With popcorn confetti, they're having a ball.
A heart can be silly, when alone in the groove,
Making up jests with each silly move.

Echoes of a Unified Soul

In a room where silence takes a bold stance,
Two hearts strike a pose, daring to dance.
Pajama party vibes, with pillows to toss,
They paint the night bright, no room for loss.

With echoes of giggles bursting in air,
They sing off-key tunes without a single care.
Together they're awkward, yet oh so divine,
Finding the fun in each silly line.

Tapestry of Emotional Echoes

In a world of tangled strings,
Laughter dances, sweetly sings.
Each thread a giggle, twist, and twist,
In this fabric, no chance is missed.

A mishap here, a chuckle there,
In the tapestry, we all share.
With each knot, a story grows,
Tickling hearts, it never slows.

Notes in the Space Between

Plucking chords on a sunny day,
Fingers slipping, it's never gray.
A melody that goes askew,
Makes everyone dance like a kangaroo.

In the gap, a rubber chicken,
Each laugh is like the clock tickin'.
With a wink and a silly pout,
We find harmony, there's no doubt.

Lullabies of the Forbidden

Ssshh... secrets wrapped in whispers,
Chocolate cake and wild-time twisters.
Singing softly with a wink,
Dreams of pranks make the mind think.

Under blankets, giggles blend,
With each hush, let's pretend.
That the rules were made to break,
And mischief's the sweetest cake.

A Chorus for Every Individual

One voice croaks, another hums,
Each note brings out the funny drums.
With harmonies made from silly truths,
We all share our travails of youth.

In the crowd, a trumpet snores,
While a clown dances across the floors.
United, we find a punchline spark,
In the chorus, we leave our mark.

Rippled Waves of Mutual Yearning

In a sea of shared desires,
We paddle round like playful choirs.
Each splash a giggle, every wave a cheer,
Floating on laughter, don't you fear!

A tug on my board, oh what a prank,
Riding the tide, we'll never tank.
With jokes like anchors, we'll never sink,
And as we bob, we nod and wink.

Seagulls squawking, adding to the fun,
We trade silly faces under the sun.
As saltwater tickles our toes and feet,
We dance on the waves, it's quite the feat!

Now we're surfing the crest of joy,
Like kids with a brand-new toy.
In this ocean of whims, we bond and play,
With rippled laughter, we rule the day.

Chorus of Eternal Companionship

Two voices blend in perfect tune,
Our jokes orbit like the moon.
A harmony of chuckles fills the air,
With giggles that float like a fluffy chair.

Dancing like socks that lost their mates,
We stumble and trip in silly fates.
Each fall a new verse in our tune,
Silly serenades under the afternoon.

Every pun we toss, oh what a show,
Like ping-pong balls, we volley and go.
Through bursts of laughter, our spirits soar,
In a duet of joy, we forever explore.

With silly hats and mismatched shoes,
In this goofy rhythm, we'll never lose.
Together we sing of friendship bold,
In the chorus of life, pure happiness unfolds.

Fusion of Hearts in Serenade

Our hearts collide in a playful dance,
With mischief in every daring chance.
Like an accordion, we stretch and squeeze,
Creating a tune that's sure to please.

With tickles and teases, we harmonize,
Eye rolls and snorts, the best surprise.
We jive through life, a quirky flow,
What else can bloom from such a show?

Banana peels and silly hats,
Life's little jokes are where we're at.
With a wink and a nudge, we drive the beat,
In this jam-packed world, we simply can't be beat.

Each note a burst of joy and cheer,
Crafting memories that we hold dear.
Together we sing in this grand parade,
The tune of our friendship, a lovely charade.

Solitary Notes in Collective Song

I whistled a tune, out of tune for sure,
A solo act that needed more.
But then came you with a silly grin,
Together we laugh, let the fun begin.

Like socks that vanish in the wash,
We're unpredictable, but never posh.
In the echo of laughter, we find our way,
A cacophony of joy, come what may.

You play the kazoo, I bang the pot,
Creating music that hits the spot.
Each silly note, a link we share,
In this zany symphony, hang on to your chair!

So let's harmonize in the dishpan choir,
With quips and giggles, we never tire.
In our melody, confusion is key,
Two silly souls, forever free!

Layers of a Singular Emotion

My heart wears socks, a polka dot pair,
It dances to beats that float in the air.
With every thump, it thinks it's a drum,
Bouncing to laughter, oh what a fun!

When feelings pile up like pancakes in stacks,
Each layer a story, with fluffy quirks and hacks.
Whipped cream and sprinkles add joy to the feast,
This heart's a dessert that never will cease.

Sometimes it stumbles, a clumsy old shoe,
Twirling around, oh what else could it do?
With each little giggle that floats to the skies,
My heart jokes about love, with laughter that flies.

In the circus of feelings, a clown takes a bow,
Wearing big shoes, it's no time for a vow.
Just chuckles and chuckles, that's the game here,
A heart so quirky brings everyone cheer.

Pulse of One-ness

Beats like a drummer who's lost in delight,
Jumping and jiving and into the night.
My heartbeat's a dance floor, shoes all askew,
Two left feet shuffling, oh where did they go?

One-two-three-four, let's loop it around,
A silly right-spin to the sink of a sound.
Every pulse giggles, a skip and a hop,
Together we're tripping, but never will stop!

In sync like a band that plays just for fun,
With kazoo and accordion, we're never outdone.
A waltz with a whoopee, a twist with a grin,
Feel the halo of laughter and let the joy in.

As we hum through the day, in our zany charade,
No need for a partner, this rhythm won't fade.
When playing our hearts like a magical game,
It's laughter that conquers, no need for a name.

Harmonies of Introspection

Plucking old notes from the strings of my mind,
A melody winks, leaving worries behind.
Composers of chaos and whimsy, we play,
Strumming on heartstrings, the echoes sway.

Inside this odd symphony, laughter comes first,
With hiccups and giggles that bubble and burst.
Each note a little twinkle that jigs on my head,
Making old worries dance away instead.

A chorus of quirks in the back of my brain,
Where logic's a jester that prances in rain.
With every reflection, a joke just in time,
Turning serious sadness to whimsical rhyme.

I'll serenade shadows with joy and odd cheer,
A duet of nonsense, the silly sincere.
In each harmony crafted with smiles as my art,
I'll sing to the madness, a true work of heart.

Cadence of a Shared Experience

Two hearts are playing hopscotch in sync,
With laughter that bubbles and purple hearts ink.
Jumping from joy to collide in a mess,
Our giggles go viral, oh, what a success!

We're partners in pranks and silly charades,
Building a castle with colorful blades.
Every shared moment is a pie in the face,
With whipped cream disaster as joy takes its place.

Dancing through moments like it's ballet, oh yes,
Twisting and twirling, it's truly a test.
When two become one in this merry parade,
Laughter's our banner, and joy won't degrade.

At dusk when the lights of our friendship ignite,
We echo our laughter into the night.
For in this great journey of giggles and cheer,
A shared goofy moment is perfectly clear.

Harmonies from Within

In a world of bouncing shoes,
We giggle as we sway,
Our hearts play silly tunes,
No worries lead astray.

With each tickle of a beat,
We stumble, trip and glide,
Our laughter sounds so sweet,
Together, side by side.

A jig to clumsy rhymes,
We dance in playful grace,
Footsteps in funny times,
A smile on every face.

Let's sing our off-key notes,
Unraveled, wild, and free,
With every hop and float,
Creating our symphony.

The Dance of One Essence

A chicken crossed the floor,
In rhythm with a cat,
They twirled and laughed some more,
What a curious spat!

With waltzes made of cheese,
And pirouettes of pie,
We dance upon the breeze,
While ice cream scoops fly high.

Funky moves from the ducks,
As frogs join in the fun,
To laugh at silly clucks,
Beneath the warming sun.

In jolly harmony,
We jig along the grass,
Embracing life's folly,
As all our worries pass.

Cadence of Connection

Bouncing like a rubber ball,
We're stuck in this fine chase,
With every giggle's call,
Our joy we can't erase.

A twist, a whirl, we spin,
Collecting laughter's spark,
With each funny grin,
We dance beneath the dark.

Like noodles in a pot,
Our rhythm starts to flare,
Entangled in this plot,
Where we all breathe rare air.

From mishaps to delight,
We sway in bumpy grace,
In chaotic flight,
We find our happy place.

Unison in Silence

We waddle like some geese,
As silence plays its game,
With goofy looks at peace,
Yet nothing feels the same.

In whispers loud as bells,
We dance without a cue,
While joking stories swell,
In worlds both bright and blue.

With every wink we share,
Our hearts take on a spree,
Connecting in mid-air,
Just you, the stars, and me.

As quiet laughter rings,
And fancies take their flight,
With silly little things,
We embrace the night.

Vibration of a Singular Intent

A single drum, it starts to beat,
With wobbly legs, we tap our feet.
A dance-off in a tiny room,
As socks slide swiftly, we all zoom!

One twirl, a spin, a giggling fall,
We laugh so loud, we wake the wall.
The ceiling shakes with joyful tone,
As heartbeats join, we're never alone.

We skip and hop on wobbly chairs,
Pretend to fly like silly bears.
A symphony of clumsy cheers,
With every note, we conquer fears!

In this odd dance, we're quite the sight,
Like rubber chickens in pure delight.
One heart, many giggles, we embrace,
In this wild beat, we've found our place.

One Heart, Many Verses

A joke's a song, and laughter's key,
Each punchline flutters, wild and free.
In a secret mood, we start to rhyme,
With each line drummed, we go in time.

Coffee spills, oh what a scene!
As humor breaks the morning sheen.
We scribble verses on our hands,
As if our selves were rockstar bands!

The echo of our playful tease,
Turns serious times to gentle breeze.
A mingled sound of boisterous cheer,
Making thoughts of worries disappear.

So gather close, let laughter grow,
In this odd dance, we steal the show.
Each giggle spins a tale so bright,
In joy, we find our shared delight.

Notes Played in Solitude

A note is struck, but who's at play?
With floppy hats and flies, hooray!
In solitude, we sing our tune,
With echoes bouncing to the moon.

A kazoo wails, a whistle squeaks,
We mimic jazz with funny peaks.
In this solo, we all collide,
Creating laughter we cannot hide.

The cat joins in, all wide-eyed,
As we compose, it seems it tried.
We share a bond of silly sound,
In quiet rooms, pure joy is found.

So let's embrace this quirky art,
In notes and stretches, we do impart.
A melody of hugs and cheer,
In solitude, it's love we steer.

The Silent Song of Weaving Souls

In whispers soft, we thread a line,
A tapestry where hearts align.
With needle pricks and thread so bright,
We stitch our giggles into the night.

Each shared moment, a colorful spin,
We weave our jokes, let the fun begin!
Through every laugh, a fiber born,
Creating warmth from souls all torn.

So take a stitch, or tie a knot,
As we create what can't be bought.
In every pattern, friendship flows,
In silly stitches, our laughter grows.

The fabric sings, both loud and sweet,
In woven joy, we dance on feet.
Together, we craft this quirky seam,
A silent song, a happy dream.

Cadence of Two Becoming One

Two left feet tripping in sync,
A dance of squirrels, what do you think?
Bouncing in tune, it's a sight to see,
Like pasta flinging wildly on spaghetti spree.

Jumping and spinning, we stumble and fall,
Catching each other, we laugh through it all.
A duet of chaos, yet so much fun,
A cacophony made, but we can't outrun.

Finding our groove with socks on the floor,
Sliding and gliding right out the door.
With every misstep, we cheer and we grin,
Together we twirl, till the madness begins.

In this funny tango, we find our way,
A silly waltz that lasts all day.
Two hearts colliding in joyous delight,
Turning mishaps to giggles, oh what a sight!

Symphony of Interwoven Souls

Our song is a mashup, strange but divine,
An owl hooting along with the pine.
A duck quacking out a beat for the bass,
Where quirky notes glide, we find our place.

With spoons and pots, we create quite a sound,
Banging on beams, we dance all around.
Puppies are howling, they join in the fun,
While we make music 'til the day is done.

In this orchestra of laughter and play,
We hit every note in our own goofy way.
It's a jolly crescendo, no need for a score,
Just joyous harmony we can't help but adore.

So tune in your ears to this splendid delight,
A symphony silly, that dances in flight.
With every wrong note, we find it's all right,
As we serenade stars shining oh so bright!

Vibrations of a Shared Essence

In the bubble of life, we bounce and we sway,
With giggles erupting in the silliest way.
A wave of laughter, a roll on the floor,
Echoing jokes that we can't ignore.

Like ducks in a row, we waddle on through,
Sharing a wink as we concoct a brew.
The potion is laughter, the secret so plain,
As we work together, we've got no disdain.

With each funny story, our vibrations align,
Filling the air with a sparkle and shine.
The joy that we share is a riotous tune,
Dancing through life, like a bright, merry moon.

It's the essence of fun, wrapped in a glance,
Where giggles burst forth in a wild, crazy dance.
With shadows and echoes transforming the night,
We find in each moment, pure delight!

Lullabies Beneath the Surface

Under the waves, the fish sing a tune,
As crabs clap their claws to a drumming balloon.
Starfish twirl in a dance, oh so grand,
While turtles surprise with a jazz band.

With bubbles that float up, we giggle and play,
Tickling seaweed in our underwater ballet.
We whisper to dolphins, our secrets to share,
Creating a chorus of joy everywhere.

Sardines shimmy, they thump and they cheer,
While jellyfish jingle without any fear.
Under the moonlight, the ocean takes part,
Crashing the surface, a splash in the heart.

It's a whimsical world where laughter is found,
In melodies swaying, and rhythms abound.
So, float with me softly, beneath the cool tide,
Where lullabies linger and silliness glides!

Chiming Hearts in Perfect Accord

Two clocks tick tock in shared delight,
Joking about who'll win the fight.
They giggle in sync, a quirky show,
Tickling time with a dance, oh so slow.

Laughter echoes in the hallway's maps,
As each heartbeat skips and taps.
It's a comedy of timing, oh what a rush,
In this silly rhythm, we gently blush.

Ticklish tones that blend and mix,
A tick-tock tune that plays little tricks.
Each chime is made to tease and poke,
In this merry duet, all worries choke.

Together we bounce, a hilarious tune,
Under the glow of the silly moon.
Harmony's laughter is sweet and bright,
In our jingling hearts, love takes flight.

Strumming the String of Togetherness

Two guitars strum silly, side by side,
Fingers fumble, and laughter won't hide.
Off-key notes create a joyful spark,
Like a love song sung by a playful lark.

Each strum a giggle, each pause a snort,
An orchestra formed of chaotic sport.
Plucking at heartstrings, oh what a feat,
In this comedy club, we take our seat.

Dancing along with a wrong-footed leap,
In the silly sound, our secrets we keep.
Every chord a chuckle, every note a play,
Making music of life in the funniest way.

A symphony forged in mismatched bliss,
In every mistake, we find a kiss.
Strumming and humming, all things align,
In this jolly jam, our hearts intertwine.

A Single Beat of Endless Euphoria

One heart beats loud, but it stumbles a bit,
Tripping on love like a comic skit.
With each silly thud, it dances about,
Wobbling joyfully, there is no doubt.

Tickle my heartstrings, give it a twang,
Let laughter erupt like a joyful clang.
As it bounces and skips in playful delight,
This heart, oh so funny, feels just right.

In the pulse of joy, we spin and we sway,
With chuckles and giggles, we lighten the day.
Each beat is a punchline, hilarious and sweet,
In our comedic duet, we find our heartbeat.

Together we leap, in sync we may fall,
With laughter resounding, echoing call.
One single beat, endless as the sky,
In our whimsy of love, we soar and we fly.

Dichotomy of Pulsing Unity

Two hearts collide like bumper cars,
Laughing at fate beneath the stars.
One goes left and the other goes right,
In the chaos of love, we find our light.

A pulsing beat that teases the air,
With every misstep, we laugh without care.
Lost in the dance of a comic embrace,
In this quirky romance, we find our place.

Heartbeat whispers in a fumbled reply,
As we trade silly glances, oh me, oh my!
Unity blooms in the loudest of glee,
Like a pair of clowns in a grand jubilee.

In our odd little waltz, we jump and we spin,
With every beat laughing, we're bound to win.
Dichotomy's pulse is a vibrant fest,
In the heart of hilarity, we find our rest.

Pulses Entwined in Time

In the café where we meet,
Your coffee spills on my feet.
We laugh and dance in our chair,
Two hearts in a clumsy affair.

Tick-tock of the clock agrees,
As we both share crumbs of cheese.
We juggle dreams, a cheesy pie,
While sipping soda, oh my my!

Hop, skip, jump – we twirl about,
You chased me once, I had to pout.
With giggles bursting, we fly high,
Like balloons escaping the sky.

Our pulses race with silly games,
Playing charades, calling names.
Each wink a spark, a funny tune,
Let's dance and sing beneath the moon.

Unison of Resounding Feelings

A sandwich shared, oh what a sight,
You ate my half, but that's alright.
With lettuce flying, a grand debate,
How two can munch, we contemplate.

Our laughter echoes through the air,
Like rubber chickens everywhere.
You tried a juggle, dropped it quick,
Yet in that moment, heartbeats tick.

We sing off-key, on purpose now,
A talent show, we'll take a bow.
With every note, a chuckle grand,
Funky moves, oh isn't it planned?

A hip-hop skip towards the sun,
Counting fails, but still we run.
In every blunder, something sweet,
Together we make life a treat.

Dances of a Beating Heart

Two left feet but we forge ahead,
You step on mine, but I'm not dead.
Twisting, turning, a funny sight,
We groove to tunes, a pure delight.

With every spin, my hat flies high,
Twirling my hair, I start to cry.
For laughter spills, and joy unwinds,
In silly dances, love's true finds.

You stomp your feet, I leap and laugh,
A crazy couple, a silly half.
Bumping and giggling, what a show,
Our hearts in sync, stealing the glow.

Each little slip, we give a cheer,
For every faff brings us more near.
So let's dance on till the sun sets,
With silly moves, no regrets yet!

Whispered Lovesongs in Sync

In the market, you sing aloud,
I try to blend in with the crowd.
My voice cracks, but you don't mind,
Your laughter's sweet, of the best kind.

Ceramics fall, a clatter's sound,
Our love's a jest; we know no bounds.
Picking up shards, sharing a grin,
In every heart, a chance to win.

With quirky phrases, our tales align,
Each whispered jest, a perfect rhyme.
We scribble notes on napkin scraps,
Our scribbles dance like playful chaps.

As evening glows with candle lights,
We share our dreams through chuckled sights.
Two souls in sync, what a fun spree,
Our whispered songs, eternally free!

Ubuntu in Melodic Silence

In a room filled with laughter,
We all dance without sound.
Knees knocking together,
We're lost but still found.

With each awkward shuffle,
Our toes start to play.
The music's in chaos,
Yet we groove anyway.

Toasting with silence,
While the snacks disappear.
Giggles fill the breezes,
As we sip from thin air.

In this joyful oddity,
We spin and we whirl.
Melodies unspoken,
As we all lose our twirl.

Vision of Heartfelt Unity

In matching pajamas,
We strut down the hall.
Our hearts beat together,
Yet we trip, fall, and crawl.

We raise empty glasses,
And toast to our team.
The laughter erupts,
Like a wild, vivid dream.

A chorus of hiccups,
Makes our cheeks turn bright.
United in giggles,
With each silly light bite.

A tapestry woven,
Of snorts and delight.
We may not be perfect,
But this feels just right.

The One Beat You Hear

In a crowded café,
We hum our own tune.
But nothing's in harmony,
Like a goose in a balloon.

We tap out a cadence,
On sugar-sticky trays.
The coffee cups rattle,
In our quirky ballet.

A cat walks a tightrope,
As we cheer with loud yelps.
Its missteps are laughter,
And so are our pelts.

With crumbs on our faces,
And joy in our hearts,
The beat that we're sharing,
Is a melody of parts.

Vows in a Singular Cadence

Two friends in a circle,
With pinky promises made.
We swear to share snacks,
And never to fade.

With spaghetti and meatballs,
Our vows turn to cheer.
As we slurp like wild bandits,
Let's toast with a leer!

In a quirky confession,
We pledge jest and great fun.
For every lost battle,
There's laughter to be won.

In sync like a turtle,
As we tumble and sway.
Bonded by giggles,
Forever we'll play.

Voices of an Unseen Beat

When the cat dances to the tune,
I can't help but laugh at the moon.
A squirrel runs with a wiggly tail,
Every limb flapping, like a cartoon fail.

The coffee spills in a lively jig,
My heart skips, so full and big.
Each tick-tock finds a quirky line,
While my socks perform, feeling fine.

A cha-cha with the wayward shoe,
Finding partners in the unexpected dew.
Two left feet still take a chance,
For every beat deserves a dance.

In whispers of laughter, we all sway,
Joining hands in this playful ballet.
Even the walls join in the fun,
Echoing the melody of everyone!

Tempo of the Heart's Whisper

Tickle my funny bone, make it sing,
A rubber chicken starts to swing.
With each heartbeat, we clown around,
A symphony of giggles abound.

The toaster pops like a cheerleader's shout,
Bread does a jig, and it's no doubt.
In this kitchen, we hold the show,
With buttered tunes and laughter's flow.

From pencils that dance on the table's edge,
To coffee mugs that wiggle and pledge.
A snicker here, a cheer over there,
Life is a stage—we're nearly a pair!

A jazz band of socks begins to roam,
Finding excitement in every home.
With a wink and a nudge, let's not be shy,
For joy is the reason, let spirits fly!

Intertwined in a Soft Serenade

In the breeze, a silly tune plays,
A dog in a tutu claims its praise.
Each bark is a note, a comedic sight,
As squirrels put on their acrobatic flight.

The telephone rings with a familiar joke,
My plant joins in, and it starts to poke.
Together we sway with our leafy refrain,
While I laugh at the drips from the rain.

A cupcake wobbles like it's had too much,
As I twirl with the spatula, it's quite the touch.
Every sprinkle sparkles in a funny way,
Each giggle inflates our hearts' ballet.

Together we gather, a comical crew,
To serenade laughter, just me and you.
With puns and pitter-patters, we easily roam,
For in fun, we've found our cozy home.

Melodic Strokes of an Endless Journey

On the bus, I catch the beat,
As old men sing in mismatched feet.
A cat throws a curveball, rolls a dice,
Every stop a stage, every glance precise.

Chasing after the ringing bell,
We giggle so hard, it's hard to tell.
With a stretch and a yawn, the bus rolls on,
In this melody, boredom's long gone.

The pigeons give tips with their noisy coo,
A tap-dance lesson? Well, maybe a few!
With each heartbeat, our quirks ignite,
Creating a concert under the streetlight.

In the end, we'll laugh and cheer,
For this journey of joy can never veer.
With a wink and a punchline, hold on tight,
The music of life, oh, what a delight!

Flowing with One Voice

We all sing from the same page,
With voices high, we fill the stage.
A cat howls, a dog barks loud,
Yet somehow, we still feel proud.

We waltz in mismatched shoes,
Tripping over our own good news.
A penguin leads a merry dance,
While we all give it a chance.

In harmony, we swerve and sway,
A chorus formed in bright dismay.
Our laughter echoes, oh what fun,
As we twist 'til the day is done.

Embrace the notes, both sharp and flat,
Together we create a chat.
So let's delight in every voice,
Life's a tune, we rejoice!

In the Quiet Cadence

In the stillness, we exchange glances,
Making jokes and silly dances.
A wink here, a nudge there,
We laugh away our rightful care.

A moment passed, a quirky sigh,
As grandma tries to leap up high.
With rhythm awkward, but hearts so light,
We sway and giggle, what a sight!

In quiet beats, we share our dreams,
Even if they burst at the seams.
A hush falls, then erupts with glee,
As we smile at our grand esprit.

Just like the clock that ticks away,
Our joy, it simply cannot sway.
With every pause, a punchline waits,
The best of moments, love creates.

Dance of the Inner Universe

In a galaxy of wobbly stars,
We're dancing to the beat of Mars.
A cosmic jig, a funny waltz,
In this expanse, we find our fault.

With planets spinning, heads in a twist,
Our silly quirks, we can't resist.
Aliens laugh at our Earthly ways,
As we stomp through our awkward phase.

The moon chuckles, the sun bursts bright,
As we twirl around with sheer delight.
From twinkling stars to dust below,
We cha-cha through life, stealing the show!

So leap aboard this rhyming ride,
With silly notions as our guide.
In the universe's vast embrace,
We find our joy, our saving grace.

Euphony of Connection

In a chat that makes no sense,
Words bouncing off like a tall fence.
We giggle, snort, and play along,
In this jumbled, silly song.

Our thoughts collide like playful bees,
Buzzing round with perfect ease.
A hodgepodge of laughter is our aim,
Every mix-up fuels the game.

Connections form in the quirkiest ways,
Like socks that dance during lazy days.
With every twist, our bond is tight,
As we spark joy like stars at night.

So grab a friend, and let's go wild,
In this laughter, we'll be beguiled.
Together we'll make a joyful sound,
In this euphonic love we've found.

Chords of a Shared Dream

In the land of mismatched socks,
Where laughter dances, and time ticks slow,
We strum the strings of silly clocks,
As giggles bloom, where wild thoughts flow.

We play a tune with jumbled beats,
Like cats in hats and frogs on skis,
Our melodies are quite the feats,
A symphony of sneezes and wheezes.

Balloons float by, all red and blue,
While cake erupts like springtime blooms,
A circus trick of nuts and stew,
In dreams where all the chocolate foams.

So take my hand, let's craft a spark,
With harmonies of ticklish fun,
Together, we will leave our mark,
In laughter's glow, we both are one.

Sonnet of the Beating Heart

My heart is like a bouncy ball,
It hops and skips, a joyful sight,
With every thump, I hear the call,
To dance beneath the moon at night.

With every squeeze, my giggles soar,
Like popcorn popping in a pan,
I wonder what my heart's for sure,
Maybe it's to laugh or maybe ban.

It thuds and shakes with every joke,
As butterflies do silly flips,
In a world where silly's bespoke,
Let's twirl like candy on our trips.

Oh, what a waltz of beats we make,
In every pulse, a reason to wake!

Whispers of Inner Peace

In my mind, a squirrel plays chess,
He ponders seriously for a nut,
While the leaves laugh in a soft caress,
And the breeze hums tunes that go 'cut, cut'.

I close my eyes to hear the fun,
A parade of thoughts, so wild and bold,
As clouds wear pajamas, laughing, spun,
In a dreamscape of joy, all untold.

The sun winks like a playful muse,
While shadows jump and play a prank,
We chase our giggles, no time to lose,
In this canvas of laughter, we're blank.

With every chuckle, peace unfolds,
In a world where dreams are made of gold.

Flow of a Single Life

Life's like a river, full of bends,
With rubber ducks and wise old fish,
It twists and turns, and never ends,
In a splash of joy, fulfill each wish.

With a hop on logs and dodging ducks,
I dance on ripples, sing in the rain,
Chasing bubbles, with all my luck,
And laughing hard till I feel no pain.

The sun shines bright, a cheeky flame,
With quirky shadows that love to play,
In the current, I make my name,
With every giggle, I sway away.

So here I float, free as a kite,
In this single life, a joyful flight.

Heartbeat Harmonies

Bouncing beats from here to there,
We dance like ants in sticky air.
A thump, a bump, a silly noise,
Our laughter rings, oh what a choice!

We skip, we hop, we twist and twirl,
Like jellybeans in a crazy whirl.
Each heartbeat sends a joke around,
We giggle, wiggle, joy unbound!

Our pulses play a playful tune,
Bouncing under the light of the moon.
With every skip, we share a grin,
In this odd rhythm, we find our kin!

So let us jump on this wild beat,
With each heartbeat, our bonds repeat.
Through giggles shared and dances bold,
We find the joy that never gets old!

Echoes of a Unified Pulse

A thump and then a clap, how grand!
We shake our fists while taking a stand.
The echoes bounce off every wall,
With each loud thud we have a ball!

A united beat, a silly cheer,
With every noise, we draw them near.
It's chaos, laughter, all in sync,
In this mad dance, we hardly think!

We share our quirks like a funky tune,
And prance around under the big balloon.
Our hearts collide, a comical sight,
In this united pulse, we take flight!

When we bump, we grin, we croon,
Echoing laughter from morning to noon.
Together we're quirky, weird, and free,
In this comical symphony, just you and me!

Melodies of a Singular Being

There's a melody in every sneeze,
A hiccup here makes one weak in knees.
With every cough, a cackle burst,
We share our tunes, oh how they cursed!

A symphony of snorts and cheers,
We play right on through joyful tears.
With clanging pots and pans galore,
Our melody's a hilarious roar!

We hum, we laugh, it's all a game,
Each quirky note we all can claim.
The soundbox here is quite absurd,
With every crack, our joy converted!

So whistle, rap, or sing out loud,
In this odd tune, we are so proud.
Together we blend in silly style,
Creating laughter that lasts a while!

Serenade of a Singular Soul

Oh the serenade we sing so sweet,
With every twirl, we stomp our feet.
A giggle here, a wink right there,
In this wild dance, no room for despair!

Each step a joke, each round a laugh,
We're mixing joy like a crazy craft.
As we sway and sway, our spirits soar,
With every encounter, we want more!

Our hearts collide like jolly drums,
Creating beats as laughter comes.
Silly moments light the way,
In this serenade, we seize the day!

So let's jiggle and laugh without fear,
In this singular tune, our hearts draw near.
Together we're strong, quite a delight,
With each note shared, we shine so bright!

Serenade of the Silent Beat

In the quiet of the night, just me and my snacks,
I heard my stomach rumble, plotting little attacks.
The moon decided to dance, with stars on parade,
While I tried to find rhythm in this feast that I made.

A cat jumped on the table, playing like a pro,
I laughed at the chaos, like a late-night show.
The pizza looked offended, the cake was in shock,
As I waltzed with my plate, like a seasoned rock.

So here's to the minutes, that pass oh so slow,
When laughter fills the air, and silliness can grow.
It's a ball in this heart, with beats out of time,
And even the oddest tunes can still sound sublime.

In the end, it's simple, we're just here for the fun,
With bites and with giggles, till the party is done.
So raise your fork high, let's celebrate the mess,
In the serenade of silence, we find our success.

Tides of One's Heart

Waves of laughter crash, in the confines of the mind,
Bobbing up like dolphins, with humor intertwined.
Each giggle is a ripple, in the ocean so vast,
A beach ball of feelings, that floats and goes past.

The tide comes in with jokes, that tide can be quite bold,
They tickle every funny bone, stories to be told.
A crab wearing a top hat, struts across the sand,
Inviting all the seagulls to join the dance so grand.

When the sun dips low, and shadows start to play,
We'll ride the waves of laughter, till the end of the day.
With buckets full of puns, and a shovel full of fun,
Dancing in the moonlight, hearts as light as the sun.

So let the waves crash onward, keep the joy in sight,
For in the tides we're surfing, every moment feels bright.
The ocean of our laughter, forever aglow,
Pulls us into rhythm, and steals the show.

Notes from the Inner Sanctuary

In the chamber of my heart, there's a piano in lace,
Each note strikes a funny chord, filling up the space.
The metronome is giggling, keeping time with flair,
As the dog joins in howling, without a single care.

The walls are lined with memories, silly moments more,
Of dancing in my pajamas, and sliding on the floor.
A vibrant tapestry woven with threads of delight,
As socks become the instruments, in our late-night fight.

A silly little ditty, on the tip of my tongue,
While the dishwasher hums along, it's a song to be sung.
So tickle the ivories gently, let the laughter flow,
In this inner sanctuary, it's a one-person show.

With the clock striking midnight, we embrace the delight,
The notes leap and spiral, into stars shining bright.
So here's to the melody, that makes our hearts sway,
In a symphony of chuckles, we dance and we play.

Interlude of an Intimate Heart

In the cozy nook of silence, my thoughts like balloons,
Float freely through the air, humming idle tunes.
A snicker from the corners, a chuckle in my chest,
The heart skips in mischief, in this joyous nest.

Between the beats, there's laughter, a catchy little strum,
Like a dance of silly shadows, it makes my heart drum.
The coffee pot is gossiping, sharing tales at dawn,
While the toast jumps in delight, with jam that's like a yawn.

So pull up to the table, let the fun unfurl,
Let's toast to little moments, that make our heads whirl.
With a wink and a nudge, we'll twirl in silly play,
In this interlude of giggles, brightening our day.

As the day turns to dusk, with light beginning to fade,
We'll treasure every chuckle, in this laughter we've made.
Here's a wink to the heart, a spark that won't depart,
In the echoes of affection, we find our funny art.

Lines from an Inner Melody

In the quiet, a drum starts to play,
Pounding beats make the cats sway.
A silly tune, the dog joins in,
Jumping and twirling, a comical spin.

The goldfish nods to the bass,
Splashing about in a watery race.
The parrot squawks with perfect flair,
Chiming in like it has a prayer.

The toaster pops, a toast to the day,
Crumbs in the air, in a ballet!
The blender joins with its whirring sound,
In this orchestra, joy is found.

So laugh with me in this wild beat,
We'll dance to a rhythm that's quite neat.
For in the chaos, we surely see,
Life's a song, just let it be!

Beats Entwined in Stillness

A turtle moves in slow, sly grace,
Raving about the world's fast pace.
His shell's a drum, he taps it right,
While birds laugh from their lofty height.

A snail joins in on this funny ride,
Spinning stories, oh, what a tide!
The ants parade, their steps so small,
Marching along their comical call.

As frogs start hopping in goofy plight,
Leaping and croaking with sheer delight.
They bring the house down, with a splash,
In this hilarious, lively bash!

So while the world holds its serious face,
Join the dance, find your own space.
For in each giggle and silly tune,
Life is better beneath the moon.

Odes of a Unified Presence

In a land where socks find their mates,
A parade of mismatches, oh, what fates!
They tango and twist, causing a scene,
Waltzing along, all in between.

The fridge hums a tune, cool and bright,
While leftovers giggle in sheer delight.
Pickles and mayo, they form a band,
Sharply conducting a sandwich strand.

Chairs start grooving, tapping their feet,
As the cat takes the lead with fancy beat.
Bouncing around, they all unite,
Creating a ruckus, what pure delight!

So raise a toast to this odd ensemble,
Together we laugh, together we ramble.
In this life where humor shines,
Every quirky heart aligns!

Cadence of a Silent Song

In the quiet of night, a sock puppet dreams,
Plotting a heist for sweet candy streams.
With a wink and a nod, it gives a shout,
Who knew socks had such a clout?

The moonlight giggles as shadows dance,
While the old cat gives her a glance.
She plans to jump, oh what a sight,
Landing right on the dog with delight!

Meanwhile, the chairs have a gossip spree,
Whispering tales of the odd TV.
The remote goes missing, oh such a mess,
Who stole it now? The couch, I guess!

So here's to the fun when silence sings,
In every corner, joy springs.
For in this world of chatter and cheer,
Let's celebrate all we hold dear!

The Quiet Symphony Within

In the silence, a tune begins to play,
Where socks dance wildly, leading astray.
A cat on a piano, quite the surprise,
Together we laugh, as the melody flies.

Tickling the ivories, a gnome takes a seat,
With a hat that's too big, but he can't feel defeat.
A sunflower and cactus join in the cheer,
While hummingbirds whistle, "Let's make this clear!"

Frogs croak the baseline, quite out of key,
Yet somehow the bubbles create harmony.
Each thump of our hearts brings a grin to our face,
As we waltz on the floor, with this quirky embrace.

In this wobbly circus, we twirl and we spin,
Our laughter pours out, where the fun will begin.
So here's to the concert of strange, silly sounds,
A joyful reminder of love that abounds.

Resonance of a Unified Beat

When timing gets funky, and life spins around,
We sway to a rhythm, a silly old sound.
A dog on a drum, what a clever encore,
Gets us laughing so hard, we can't take it anymore.

The ice cream truck's jingle, a cue for a treat,
Two kids start breakdancing, with outrageous feet.
With bananas as keyboards, we're ready to jam,
Creating a chorus that sounds like a slam.

A squirrel joins the chorus, his tail in a flip,
While bees bring the buzz in a whimsical trip.
With bees on the beat, and wild giggles on high,
We'll harmonize joy, like a pie in the sky.

So slap on your shoes and let's dance in a line,
With heartbeats as drums, we'll be just fine.
Together we waddle, we jig, and we twist,
In this laughter-filled duet, there's nothing we've missed.

Melodies Weaving Through Solitude

Alone in my room, I start to compose,
With a broom for a guitar, who knows where it goes?
The ceiling fans sway to the tune that I play,
And my pet goldfish joins in, swimming all day.

Old socks make great shakers, if you give them a shake,
While the toaster joins in with a pop and a baked.
A cucumber's the star, in a lead role so bright,
Shining under the lights, it's a vegetable night.

With each silly beat, my worries take flight,
Laughter is blooming, all feels so light.
My heart skips a beat, as I dance on my toes,
The rhythm is silly, where nobody knows.

So let's bring a giggle, a cheer, and some flair,
With laughter and music, we're beyond compare.
In this jolly adventure, we'll compose, and we'll sing,
For joy is the music, let's give it a swing.

The Language of Heartbeats

In the kitchen, a rumble, the pots start to hum,
As spoons race each other, with a clattering drum.
A happy old fridge, it's dancing with glee,
While I'm chopping up veggies, oh can't you see?

The pasta is twirling, a wonderful sight,
Got me laughing so hard, I forgot it's not right!
The cookie jar giggles, it's hiding the treats,
In this symphony joyful, where everything beats.

Who knew that a dance party starts with a pie?
The blender should join in, at least give it a try!
With spices for rhythm and frosting for flair,
Every cook is a maestro with love in the air.

So let's grab our utensils, it's time for a show,
We'll waltz to the table, not caring who knows.
With heartbeats in sync, and cookies in hand,
We'll laugh and then sing, as we carry this band.

Heartbeats of the Universe

In this wacky cosmic dance,
Stars do the cha-cha, oh what a chance!
Galaxies twirl in vibrant delight,
While comets are flashing, zooming in flight.

The planets all giggle, oh what a scene,
Mars trips on Venus, it's quite the routine!
Jupiter roars with a booming laugh,
While Saturn's rings dance in a jolly half.

Cosmic balloons float up in the air,
As nebulae twirl without a care.
The sun's got jokes, as bright as a flare,
In this universe, nothing's too rare!

So let's pulse with laughter, ignite the spark,
In this cosmic party, we share the arc.
For each twinkling star has a story to tell,
Of joyous antics, oh can't you tell?

Symphony of Silent Affection

In a quiet cafe where hearts meet and greet,
A piano plays tunes that are light on their feet.
Muffins waltz lightly on the warm table,
While teacups tap out a rhythm that's stable.

Sugar cubes giggle when dropped in the brew,
A harmony sweet, as if they just knew.
Cream swirls in circles, a ballet no less,
As spoons join together in a humorous mess.

Napkins flutter softly, a gentle ballet,
While laughter erupts in a whimsical way.
Each clink of the glass is a note played just right,
In this silent symphony, love takes flight.

So raise a toast to the giggles we share,
For in each little moment, affection is there.
With warm hearts aglow, let the music run wild,
In this funny duet, we're forever beguiled!

Unfolding the Inner Beat

Clothes in the closet have their own groove,
Socks and shirts shimmy, making us move.
Pants do the twist while jackets swing right,
In this fashion parade, what a silly sight!

Shoes tap a rhythm, not missing a beat,
While belts spin around, they're a marvelous treat.
Hats tip their brims, joining in the fun,
Clothing's a dance until the day's done.

Bags play the chorus, jingling with glee,
As scarves flutter softly, wild and free.
We're all in this wardrobe, waltzing the day,
With every small step, we're here to play.

So let's twirl in our fabric, create our own sound,
In the unfolding encore, laughter is found.
Each outfit a moment, innovative beat,
In this vibrant assembly, life's truly sweet!

Timeless Echoes of a Single Heart

Once there was a heart, quite puzzled indeed,
It echoed with thoughts of love, joy, and speed.
Bouncing like rubber, it caused quite the stir,
As it tried to find laughter, oh how it did purr!

It hummed little tunes, a quirky delight,
Making butterfly wings giggle in flight.
With every small thump, it whispered a cheer,
Cactus plants grinned, 'Oh, we love you, dear!'

The clock ticked along, counting seconds so bright,
But the heart danced a jig, making hours feel light.
Each beat a reminder of whimsy and fun,
As it bounced through the day, under warm sun.

So let's all tune in, to our own little beat,
And embrace every giggle, life's funny and sweet.
For with each wiggly laugh, a new story starts,
In the timeless echoes of our playful hearts!

Sentiments of a Shared Heart

Two friends with one weird thought,
Eating spaghetti, who knew it was fraught?
Slurping noodles at a crazy pace,
Laughter erupts, sauce all over the face.

We share our dreams on pizza slices,
Toppings debate turns into surprises.
Each cheesy laugh, a priceless score,
Like dancers on the kitchen floor.

When we cry over soap's last scenes,
Silence wraps us in silly memes.
With shared hearts we giggle and joke,
Life's a comedy, a perfect poke.

In the end, we're just two peas,
Taking life as it comes, with ease.
A wild duo, a quirky pair,
Together we dance on this crazy air.

Echoing in Perfect Harmony

With mismatched socks, we start the day,
Singing off-key, in our own ballet.
A melody of missed notes and laughs,
Dancing like ducks on silly paths.

We share the last cookie, a heated fight,
With crumbs in our hair, what a sight!
Each battle's won with a playful grin,
Love's just a game, let the fun begin!

Karaoke nights turn into grand shows,
Our voices cracking, but who really knows?
In chorus we clash, like cats and dogs,
Yet together we thrive, just two silly frogs.

So bring on the awkward and weird,
In each funny moment, we've cheered.
With hearts that beat like a drum, we find,
In laughter's embrace, we're perfectly intertwined.

The Dance of Shared Solitude

In quiet rooms, we dance alone,
Two souls grooving, each in their zone.
We twirl to silence, stomp on the floor,
With nothing but socks, who needs more?

Facing mirrors, we strike silly poses,
Arms flail wildly, like garden hoses.
Each goofy glance, a shared delight,
Lost in our worlds, we shine so bright.

Sometimes we talk to our reflections,
Crafting stories of wild connections.
With popcorn clouds and imaginary friends,
Solitude sings, and laughter never ends.

So let's embrace this funny dance,
In our oddity, we find romance.
Two hearts entwined in solo fun,
In the wacky rhythm, we have won.

Fluidity of One Heart

In chaotic moments, we find our flow,
Two hearts drift like a weird chateau.
We juggle balls, we might lose one,
With silly giggles, who needs to run?

On rollerblades with mismatched boots,
We skate through life, with giggly hoots.
Each stumble makes a funny tale,
As our laughter rides the wind like a sail.

We sip on tea, our quirks collide,
With sugar spills, we laugh and hide.
In every blunder a treasure we see,
From splashes of chaos, we're wild and free.

So let's dance through puddles, hand in hand,
In the fluid rhythm of our own band.
With an echo of laughter, a playful dart,
In every silly moment, we share one heart.

Beats Beneath the Stillness

In the quiet, a tap dance grows,
My heart's playing hide and seek with my toes.
A beat in my chest, a thump and a bump,
Who's drumming that tune? Must be my lunch's lump.

Socks slip and slide, oh what a show,
Left foot, right foot, my own little flow.
In this stillness, my heart takes flight,
A solo performance in the dead of night.

Solitary Symphony

A symphony plays, just for one,
It's a concert where I'm the lone fun.
With popcorn in hand, I tap on my knee,
Conducting the chaos with glee, just me!

The cat rolls her eyes, she's not impressed,
While I whirl and twirl, feeling blessed.
A one-man band with a spoon for a mic,
Who knew being solo was such a delight?

Chasing the Pulse Within

I chase my own pulse like it's a game,
Running in circles, but who is to blame?
The tick-tock dance in my chest goes boom,
A cardio party in my tiny room.

Sweat on my brow, let's give it a twist,
As I jiggle and wiggle, can't resist!
Heartbeat racing, what a silly chase,
There's no one to catch me in this funny space.

Vibrations of a Singular Love

The phone vibrates like my heart's new friend,
Each chime and jingle, let the fun begin!
It's not love, just spam, but I can't resist,
A dance in my chair, oh, add it to the list!

With every ping, I feel the beat rise,
Texting my snack, what a goofy surprise!
In this crazy world, I'm my own muse,
Rocking the vibes, no time to lose.

Chords of Connected Spirits

In a band of clumsy pals, we sing,
Each voice a wobbly, flappy thing.
Laughter echoes, flat notes fly,
Our offbeat joy is hard to deny.

We dance like jelly on a plate,
Trying to groove, but it's too late.
Guitar strings snap, we all just grin,
Together we play, it's fun to be kin.

On the stage, our quirks unite,
Fumbling notes, what a delight!
Our melody, a silly parade,
In this symphony, joy is made.

Through crazy chords, we find our way,
Laughing louder with each sway.
Offbeat hearts, join in the fun,
Connected always, our song's just begun.

Tapestry of Heartbeats

Once we thought we were so cool,
Now we laugh, we're just a school.
All bundled up in silly threads,
Stitching tales from our own heads.

We gather stories, some bizarre,
Like knitted cats, they travel far.
A patchwork quilt of pranks and sighs,
Creating chaos, oh my my!

With mismatched socks and polka-dots,
We celebrate with giggles and lots.
Our woven laughs make up the art,
Each knot a beat from the beating heart.

In comfy chairs, we weave and cheer,
Echoes of humor fill the sphere.
A joyful mess, this tapestry,
Bound by love and mystery.

Consort of Emotive Resonance

In the orchestra of random pranks,
We gather at the laughter banks.
Our jests and jumbles form a tune,
A cacophony by the light of the moon.

Each silly remark, a note in flight,
Chasing the shadows into the light.
With echoes that wobble and sway,
We play our hearts out, come what may.

In the concert of our clumsy charms,
We win the day with our goofy arms.
Our offbeat joy strikes a chord,
Carrying laughter, our shared reward.

As claps replace what boasts might say,
Together we dance, forever play.
This ensemble of giggles is our art,
Crafted with care by each silly heart.

The Universe Within a Pulse

In a galaxy of quirky blunders,
We orbit round with laughs like thunder.
Our hearts beat funny, a cosmic dance,
With every giggle, we take a chance.

Stars collide in a glimmering spark,
As we trip lightly and make our mark.
From silly jokes that drift and twirl,
We create a universe, a joyful whirl.

In constellations of silly smiles,
We travel far over laughter miles.
Our comet trails of playful cheer,
A cosmic symphony for all to hear.

So here we float on this funny course,
With heartbeats loud, we feel the force.
In this vast space where joy takes flight,
The pulse of laughter shines so bright.

www.ingramcontent.com/pod-product-compliance
Ingram Content Group UK Ltd.
Pitfield, Milton Keynes, MK11 3LW, UK
UKHW022104050225
454743UK00006B/69

9 783690 810234